Created by Team Campfire
Special thanks to Nandini Patodia

The shlokas in Sanskrit have been taken from ancient Indian scriptures.
The couplets in Hindi have been written by Nandini Patodia for
Kalyani Navyug Media Pvt. Ltd.
The translations in English are by Kalyani Navyug Media Pvt. Ltd.

Published by Kalyani Navyug Media Pvt. Ltd.
101 C, Shiv House, Hari Nagar Ashram,
New Delhi 110014, India

ISBN: 978-93-81182-82-6

Copyright © 2018 Kalyani Navyug Media Pvt. Ltd.

Printed in India

A *shloka* is a short verse in Sanskrit. Most Sanskrit literary works, such as the Vedas, Puranas and the epics, have been created as a collection of *shlokas*.

We are pleased to present this small collection of popular *shlokas* to help parents introduce their children to the richness of Sanskrit literary tradition. Each *shloka* has been selected from Sanskrit scripture and is dedicated to a particular god, goddess or situation. The *shlokas* are accompanied by attractive illustrations, and are presented in *devanagari*, followed by a phonetic transcription in the Latin alphabet, and a detailed explanatory translation in English.

We hope this book proves invaluable in helping create an awareness among children of the spiritual legacy of Sanskrit texts. Campfire will keep contributing to our readers' spiritual awakening by publishing more such books.

Indian Scripture

The **Vedas** are India's oldest texts that were composed in an early form of Sanskrit and then passed down orally for generations. The *Rig Veda* is the oldest of them, followed by the *Sama Veda*, the *Yajur Veda* and the *Atharva Veda*. They are mainly collections of hymns, chants, and descriptions of rituals and sacrifices. The Vedas have numerous accompanying texts such as the *Brahmanas*, *Aranyakas* and the *Upanishadas*.

The **Epics**, such as the *Ramayana* and the *Mahabharata*, are among India's richest literary creations. Every Indian knows at least the basic outline of both the epics and they are highly popular as a cultural medium among all strata of society.

Along with the epics, the **Puranas** and their tales are also extremely popular. There are 18 major Puranas, each dedicated to a particular god, and many minor Puranas.

Most of the shlokas in this book are taken from the Puranas, along with a few from the Vedas and epics.

Note on transliteration

The following is a guide to how the Sanskrit vowels, as they are presented in this book, should be pronounced:

अ	=	a
आ	=	aa
इ	=	i
ई	=	ii
उ	=	u
ऊ	=	oo
ए	=	e
ऐ	=	ai
ओ	=	o
औ	=	au

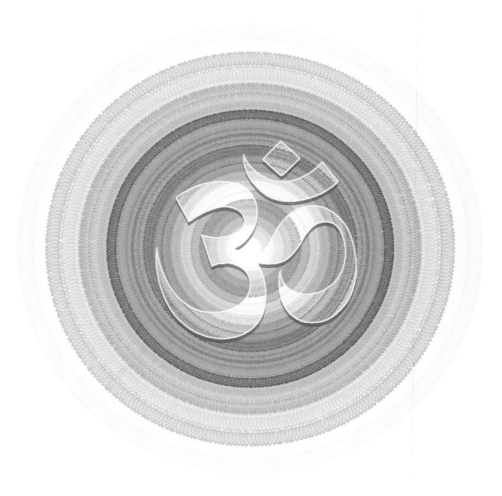

ॐ भूर्भुवः स्वः
तत्सवितुर्वरेण्यं ।
भर्गो देवस्य धीमहि
धियो यो नः प्रचोदयात् ।।

Om bhoor bhuvah svaha
Tat savi-tur va-renyam |
bhargo devasya dhii-mahi
dhiyo yo nah pracho-dayaat ||

Source: Rig Veda

The Gayatri Mantra is from the Rig Veda and is dedicated to Savitr, the Vedic Sun Deity/Source of all Life. It starts with the cosmic sound of Aum and refers to the three realms of existence – the physical (body), mental (life force) and spiritual (soul). The Sun/Creator is the One whom we worship and adore, and whose divine light permeates all three realms. The supreme Lord on whose glory we meditate, may He inspire our intellect.

त्वमेव माता च पिता त्वमेव
त्वमेव बन्धुश्च सखा त्वमेव।
त्वमेव विद्या द्रविणम् त्वमेव
त्वमेव सर्वम् मम देव देव।।

Tva-meva Maataa Cha Pitaa Tva-meva
Tva-meva Bandhush-Cha Sakhaa Tva-meva |
Tva-meva Vidyaa Dravi-nam Tva-meva
Tva-meva Sarvam Mama Deva Deva ||

Source: Pandava Gita

You are my mother and my father. You are my brother and
my friend. You are my knowledge and my wealth.
You are everything to me, my God of Gods.

गुरुर्ब्रह्मा गुरुर्विष्णुर्गुरुर्देवो महेश्वरः ।
गुरु साक्षात् परं ब्रह्म तस्मै श्रीगुरवे नमः ।।

Gurur-Brahmaa Gurur-Vishnu Gurur-devo Mahe-shvarah |
Guru Saakshaat Param Brahma Tasmai Shrii-gurave Namah ||

Source: Skanda Purana

Guru - Teacher

'Gu' means darkness, 'Ru' means light and 'Guru' is someone who removes darkness through the light of knowledge. Guru is Brahma, Vishnu and Shiva himself. Guru is the supreme teacher who gives knowledge and destroys the weed of ignorance, so we all respect and bow to him.

चूहा प्रतीक है अन्धकार का
और हमारे अहम् भाव का
उसे बनाकर वाहन गणपति
देते वर सुख, सुबुद्धि का।

The little mouse bears Ganesha,
the elephant-headed god
Who removes all obstacles, for
which him we laud.

वक्रतुण्ड महाकाय सूर्यकोटि समप्रभ।
निर्विघ्नं कुरु मे देव सर्वकार्येषु सर्वदा।।

Vakra-tund Mahaa-kaaya Soorya-koti Samap-prabha |
Nir-vighanam Kuru Me Deva Sarva-kaar-yeshu Sarvadaa ||

Source: Mudgala Purana

Ganesha - Lord of Wisdom and Remover of Obstacles

Lord Ganesha, you have a curved trunk and a large body. You have
the brilliance of a million suns. We pray to you to make us succeed
in all our daily work and remove all obstacles from our lives.

मन की चंचलता दर्शाते
सात धवल घोड़े रथ के
सूर्यदेव आसीन हो इन पर
सृष्टि को उज्जवल हैं करते।

See how on a golden
chariot the Sun God rides
Pulled by seven white horses
with such mighty strides.

आदिदेव नमस्तुभ्यं प्रसीद मम भास्कर।
दिवाकर नमस्तुभ्यं प्रभाकर नमोऽस्तु ते।।

Aadi-deva Namas-tubhyam Prasiida Mama Bhaas-kara |
Divaa-kara Namas-tubhyam Prabhaa-kara Namostu Te ||

Source: Samba Purana

Surya - Source of all Light and Energy

We pray to you O Adideva (the first amongst the Gods).
Please be kind to me O Bhaskara who sheds light all around.
Salutations to the creator of the day (Divakar), salutations to the
creator of light (Prabhakar).

जग के पालनहार विष्णु ने
चुना जिसे वाहन है
वह धीर वीर सतर्क तेजस्वी
पक्षीराज गरूड़ है।

The broad winged Garuda (eagle)
flies far and wide
As it carries Lord Vishnu
in its stride.

शान्ताकारं भुजगशयनं पद्मनाभं सुरेशं
विश्वाधारं गगनसदृशं मेघवर्णं शुभाङ्गम् ।
लक्ष्मीकान्तं कमलनयनं योगिभिर्ध्यानगम्यम्
वन्दे विष्णुं भवभयहरं सर्वलोकैकनाथम् ।।

Shaantaa-kaaram Bhujaga-shayanam Padma-naabham Suresham
Vishvaa-dhaaram Gagana-sa-drisham Megha-varnam Shubhaang-gam|
Lakshmii-kaantam Kamala-nayanam Yogibhir-dhyaana-gamyam
Vande Vishnum Bhava-bhaya-haram Sarva-lokaik-naatham ||

Source: Mahabharata

Vishnu - Lord and Preserver of the Universe

We pray to you Lord Vishnu, one who has a calm appearance and who rests on a serpent. He has a lotus on his navel and is the Lord of all the Devas (Lords). He sustains the universe and is infinite like the sky. His colour is like the clouds (blue) and he has a beautiful and auspicious body. He is the consort of Goddess Lakshmi. His eyes are like the lotus. All the yogis meditate on him. Salutations to that Lord Vishnu who removes the fear of worldly existence and who is the Lord of all the Lokas (Worlds).

शिवजी के प्रिय नंदी बैल की
महिमा बड़ी निराली है
वाहन है यह शिव शक्ति का
अद्भुत है बलशाली है।

Nandi the bull is steadfast
and strong,
And by Shiva's side he
stays, and does no wrong.

ऊँ त्रयम्बकं यजामहे सुगन्धिं पुष्टिवर्धनम्
उर्वारुकमिव बन्धनात् मृत्योर्मोक्षीय मामृतात्।।

Om Trayam-bakam Yajaa-mahe Sugandhim Pushti-vardhanam |
Urvaa-rukamiva Bandha-naat Mrityor-mokshiya Maa-mritaat ||

Source: Rig Veda

Shiva - Lord Supreme

We worship you Lord Shiva, the three-eyed one. You nourish our lives, making it fragrant, blessing us with health, wealth and well being. As a ripe fruit easily falls off its vine (is released of its bondage), may you liberate us from death and lead us towards immortality.

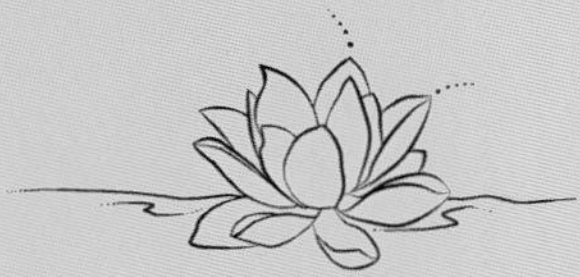

शक्तिरूप देवी दुर्गा का
वाहन पशुराज सिंह है
इसकी दहाड़ की गूँज सभी
असुरों का दिल दहलाती है।

The lion accompanies Durga, the
goddess of energy and power
And in front of them all demons
tremble in fear and cower.

सर्वमङ्गलमाङ्गल्ये शिवे सर्वार्थसाधिके।
शरण्ये त्रयम्बके गौरि नारायणि नमोऽस्तु ते।।

Sarva mangal maangalye Shive Sarvaartha saadhike |
Sharanye Trayam-ba-ke Gauri-Naaraayani Namo-stute ||

Source: Markandeya Purana

Durga - Adi Shakti, One who is divine energy Herself

You are the greatest amongst all and are the most auspicious one.
You are the consort of Lord Shiva, and are also known as Gauri and
Narayani. You, the three-eyed one, are the creator of the three
worlds, the protector of the universe and one who spreads well-being
in the cosmos. We bow down to you Mother Durga again and again.

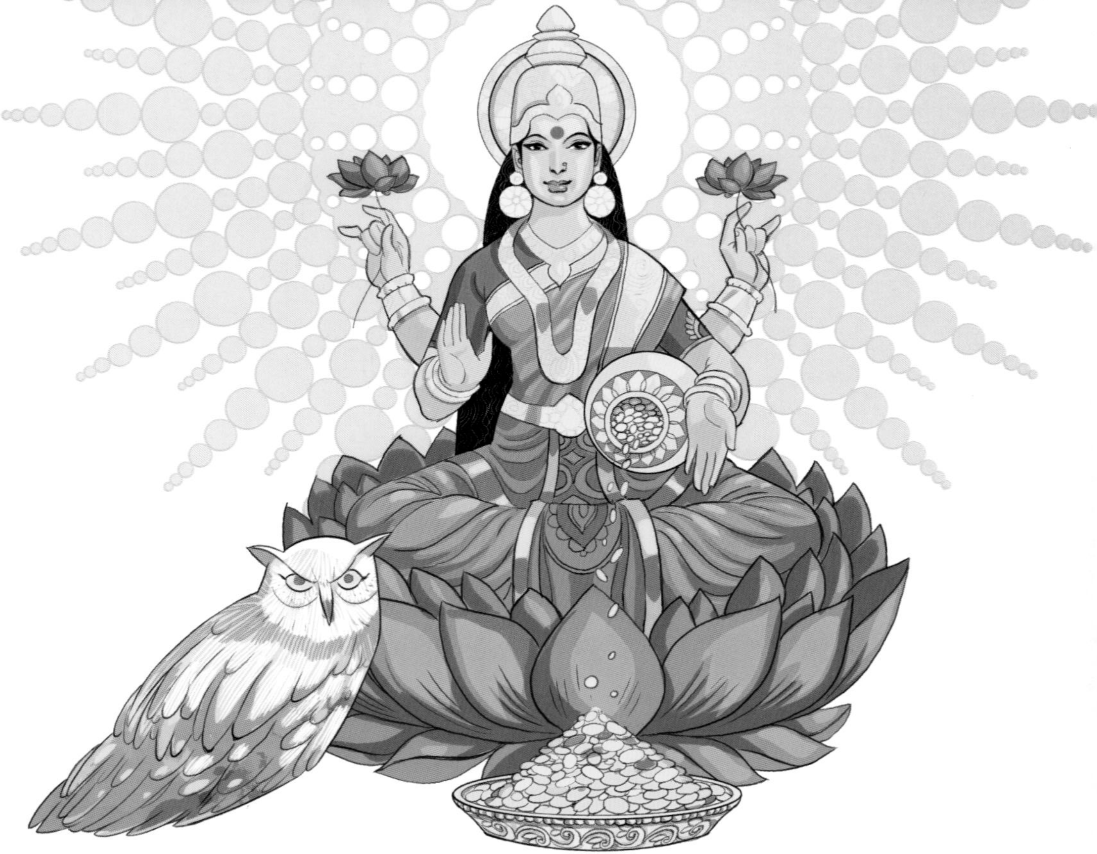

शुभ्र उलूक प्रतीक धैर्य का
विद्वत्ता और पवित्रता का
इसीलिए तो वाहन है यह
धन की देवी लक्ष्मीजी का।

The owl is beautiful and wise, and
patience is its virtue.
It accompanies Goddess Lakshmi,
who makes one's wishes of wealth
and happiness come true.

आदिलक्ष्मि नमस्तेऽस्तु परब्रह्मस्वरूपिणि।
यशो देहि धनं देहि सर्वकामांश्च देहि मे॥

Aadi-lakshmi Namas-testu Para-brahma swa-roopini |
Yasho Dehi Dhanam Dehi Sarva-kamaank-sha Dehi Me ||

Source: Mahalakshmi Stuti

Lakshmi - Goddess of Wealth and Prosperity

We pray to you Goddess Adi Lakshmi, who is the embodiment of
the Absolute. Please grant us fame, wealth, prosperity and fulfill
all our wishes.

विद्यादायिनी सरस्वती का
शुभ्र हंस है वाहन
दर्शाता है जीवन में, वही,
जो है सुंदर और पावन।

The white swan is pure,
beautiful and dazzling.
Like Saraswati, the goddess of
wisdom and learning.

सरस्वति नमस्तुभ्यं वरदे कामरूपिणि।
विद्यारम्भं करिष्यामि सिद्धिर्भवतु मे सदा।।

Sarasvati Namas tubhyam Varade Kaama-roopini |
Vidyaa-rambham Karish-yaami Siddhir-bhavatu Me Sadaa ||

Source: Saraswati Vandana

Saraswati - Goddess of Knowledge

We pray to you Mother Saraswati. You are the giver of boons and you fulfill our wishes. When I begin my learning, please bless me with the right understanding to achieve knowledge and success.

अन्धकार सा काला कौवा
दुष्ट सभी इससे डरते
वाहन है यह शनिदेव का
जो सदैव न्याय ही करते।

A black raven in the
darkness appears
When Shani's judgment is
coming near.

नीलांजन समाभासं रवि पुत्रं यमाग्रजम।
छायामार्तंड संभूतं तं नमामि शनैश्चरम।।

Niilaanjan Samaa-bhaasam Ravi Putram Yamaa-grajam |
Chhaayaa-maartand Sambhoo-tam Tam Namaami Shanai-shcharam | |

Source: Purana

Shani - Lord of Justice

He looks resplendent and majestic like a blue mountain. He is the son of Surya (Sun God) and the elder brother of Yama (God of Death). He is born to Chhaayaa and Martanda (another name of Sun God). He can even put his shadow over the glorious Sun. I bow down to the one who moves at a slow pace.

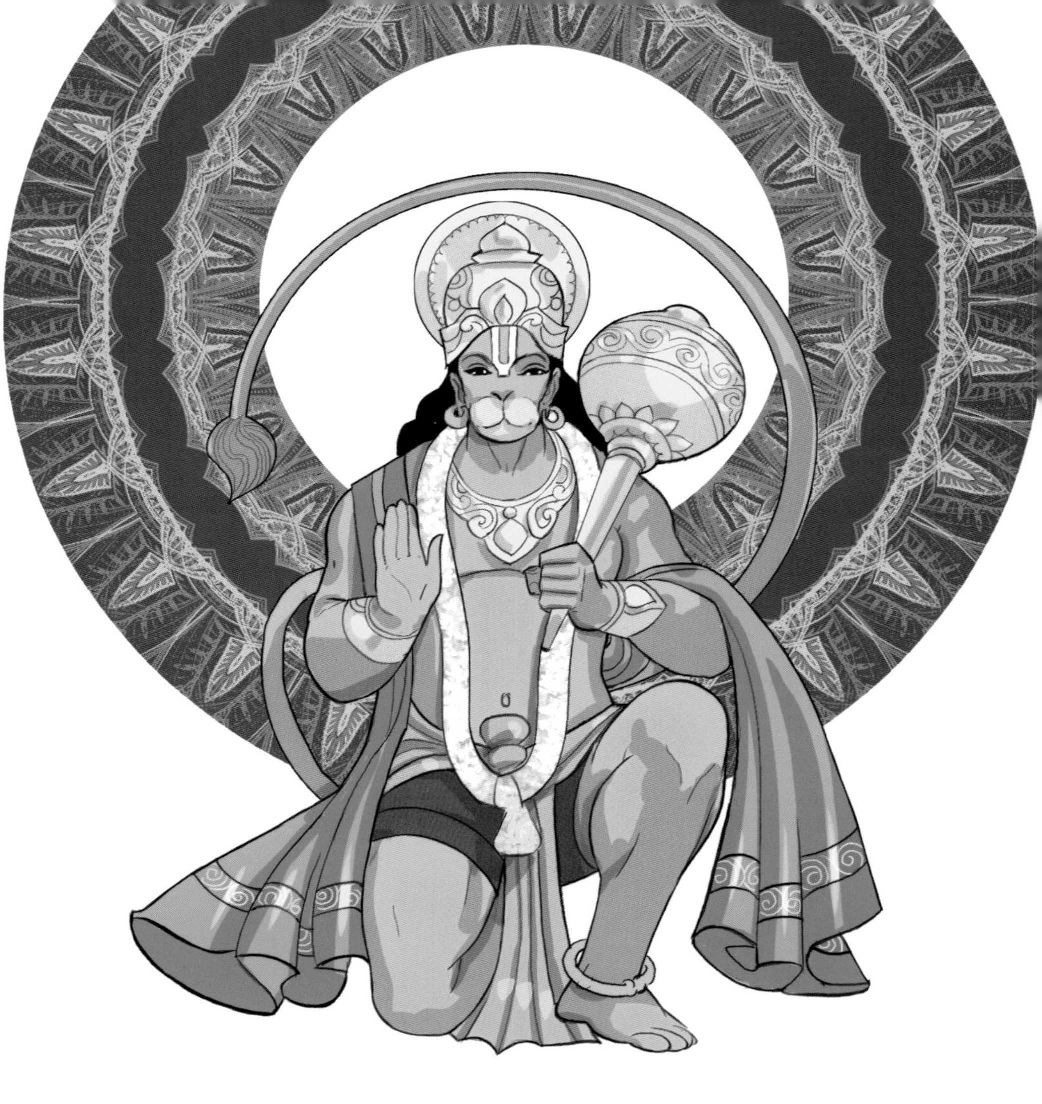

अतुलितबलधामं हेमशैलाभदेहं
दनुजवनकृशानुं ज्ञानिनामग्रगण्यम्।
सकलगुणनिधानं वानराणामधीशं
रघुपतिप्रियभक्तं वातात्मजं नमामि।।

Atulita-bala-dhaamam Hema-shailaabha-deham
Danuja-vana-krishaanum Gyaani-naam-agra-gannyam |
Sakala-guna-nidhaa-nam Vaanaraa-naam-adhii-sham
Raghupati-priya-bhaktam Vaataat-majam Namaami ||

Source: Ramayana

Hanuman - Devotee of Rama

Lord Hanuman, you have unparallel power and your huge body shines like a golden mountain. You are like a raging fire that burns the forest of demons (forces of darkness). You are the foremost amongst the wise ones and are the embodiment of all good qualities. You are the master of all monkeys (monkeys denote the mind and senses), and the dearest devotee of Lord Rama. The son of Wind God Vayudeva, we pray to you Lord Hanuman, to receive your protection.